Rain

Words by David Bennett
Pictures by Rosalinda Kightley

A BANTAM LITTLE ROOSTER BOOK™

Toronto · New York · London · Sydney · Auckland

Do you know where rain comes from?

Rain falls from the clouds in the sky.

Rainwater collects in puddles, ponds, rivers, lakes, and oceans.

Did you know that over half the world is covered by water all the time?

Warmth from the sun makes the water change into an invisible gas called water vapor.

The vapor rises into the sky.

The vapor moves higher and higher.
When the air gets very cold,
this invisible mist turns into millions
of tiny droplets of water.

The droplets stay in the air
and form a cloud.

Inside the clouds, the droplets bump into each other and join together.

They get bigger and bigger . . . .

And when they are too heavy to be held up by the air, they fall as raindrops.

The rain soaks into the ground.
Plants drink the water through
their roots. It helps them to grow
leaves and flowers.
Without rain there would be no plants.

Sometimes huge, dark clouds
crowd together overhead.
Suddenly, the day turns stormy.

Raindrops inside the storm clouds
carry electricity.
When this electricity escapes,
giant sparks called lightning
flash across the sky.

Lightning jumps from the clouds
to the earth faster than you can blink.

Lightning makes the air so hot
that it explodes with a terrific
CCRRAAAK BOOM!

This is called thunder.

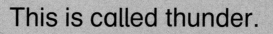

Lightning and thunder happen at
the same time.
But when things are a long way away,
you can see them before you can
hear them.
So, first you see the flash of lightning,
and then you hear the loud boom
of thunder.

Count the seconds between the
flashes of lightning and the crashes
of thunder.
If you count less each time,
the storm is coming nearer.
One, two, three . . . .

If you count more each time,
the storm is going away.
One, two, three, four, five, six . . . .

The storm has gone away.
Sunshine warms the water.
Do you know what happens next?

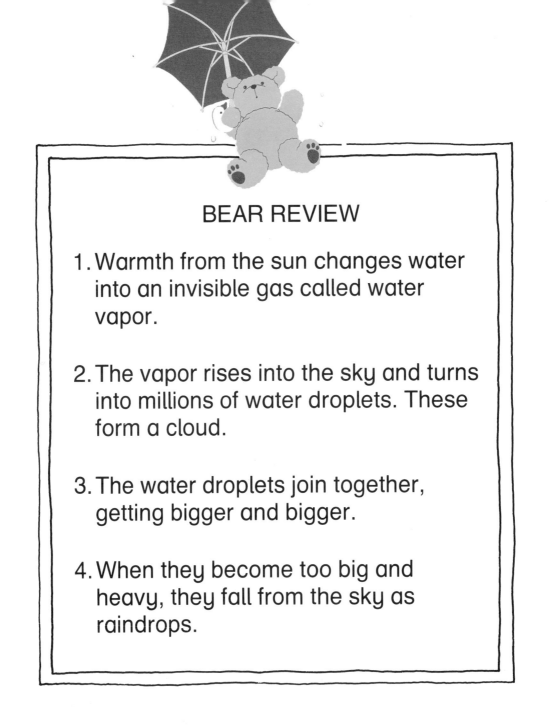

BEAR REVIEW

1. Warmth from the sun changes water into an invisible gas called water vapor.

2. The vapor rises into the sky and turns into millions of water droplets. These form a cloud.

3. The water droplets join together, getting bigger and bigger.

4. When they become too big and heavy, they fall from the sky as raindrops.